Counting Lions

Portraits from the Wild

For my darling wife, Lisa, and beautiful children,
Emily, Evie, and Archie
— S.W.

For Gus
— K.C.

Text copyright © 2015 by Frances Lincoln Children's Books
Illustrations copyright © 2015 by Stephen Walton
Foreword copyright © 2015 by Virginia McKenna
Photograph of Virginia McKenna © Andy Gotts 2012

First published in the U.K. in 2015 by Frances Lincoln Children's Books,
74–77 White Lion Street, London N1 9PF

Commissioned by Rachel Williams • Designed by Andrew Watson

First U.S. edition 2015

Library of Congress Catalog Card Number 2014957760
ISBN 978-0-7636-8207-1

15 16 17 18 19 20 CCP 10 9 8 7 6 5 4 3 2 1

Printed in Shenzhen, Guangdong, China

This book was typeset in Adobe Garamond Pro.
The illustrations were done in charcoal.

Candlewick Press
99 Dover Street
Somerville, Massachusetts 02144

visit us at www.candlewick.com

Counting Lions

Portraits from the Wild

Katie Cotton

illustrated by
Stephen Walton

with a foreword by
Virginia McKenna

CANDLEWICK PRESS

Foreword

Virginia McKenna

When you look at a picture of an animal, whether it is a photograph, a painting, or, as in this wonderful book, a drawing, words seem unnecessary. You can see the unique form and beauty of each creature in the image before you, as well as, often, the wild environment where it lives; words add little to our sense of wonder. But this book is different. It is not only showing us a lion, elephants, zebras, and turtles, but it is also asking us to count them.

In *Counting Lions,* children will start at number one and end at number ten. If it was true that there were, in reality, only five elephants or four tigers, then the world would know that the end of those species is in sight. That fearful moment has not arrived — yet. But no one can be ignorant of the fact that an increasing number of species of wild animals are part of this counting crisis. In 1900, there were 10 million African elephants. In 2014, there were 434,000 — and that number falls weekly. Just over a hundred years ago, there were about 100,000 tigers. In 2014, there were fewer than 4,000.

So why are we killing these extraordinary creatures, whose habits and behavior create the wild forests and plains and swamps that make the world so beautiful? Some people want to capture wild birds, reptiles, and primates and bring them into captivity for the pet trade. Others want to kill them for sport — trophy hunting. And a growing number of humans are demanding parts of them — a little piece of an elephant's ivory tusk, the rhino's horn, the tiger's skin and bone. The price of these animal parts is astronomical. But the price the animal pays is its life.

Increasing human populations bring about the reduction of wilderness, as cattle and goats and sheep need more and more land for grazing and humans need more areas for crop growing and housing, but there remain remote areas where wild animals are left to be themselves (although it is sadly true that many of these need full-time rangers to protect them). I have been tremendously fortunate to have traveled to several African countries and seen some of these creatures in the wild. I have heard lions roaring and birds calling, seen elephants silently moving across the plains and water buffalo disappearing in a cloud of dust, sat quietly by a swamp as myriad species of birds wade, flutter, swoop, and call. All are beautiful and all play an essential role in the creation and protection of the natural world. Each is a priceless gift. None should be taken for granted.

My hope is that this book will awaken a similar sense of wonder in all who read it and look at Stephen Walton's beautiful images — that the knowledge that animals feel contentment and sadness as we do, protect their young, sometimes are brave and sometimes afraid, will ensure that counting animals will be something we do not with a heavy heart, but with optimism and joy.

Virginia McKenna

One lion

sits and watches his rough-and-tumble pride.

He surveys the golden savanna, and a flicker catches his eye—

something moving in the grass. A challenger to his throne?

His muscles tighten. He throws back his huge head,

about to roar—but it is only a lioness, returning with a kill.

He settles down to keep watch again.

Who knows what he has seen?

One king.

One lion.

Two gorillas

breathe the same breath.
The child was born a tiny, four-pound thing of hair and bone and not much else,
so the mother keeps him close.
For two or three years, they clasp each other,
one creature, while he grows and grows and grows.
Later, as he climbs the trees alone,
he may forget they were once
two together.
Two gorillas.

Three giraffes

with their heads in the sky
pluck leaves from trees and chew,
up and down, side to side,
for up to twenty hours a day.
They are peaceful patterned giants
wandering from place to place,
sleepless surveyors of the grasslands.
Three wanderers.
Three giraffes.

Four tigers

rest in dappled shade.

The mother raises her magnificent head.

She is a warrior of the forest, heavily muscled,

a flash of fire and night that brings oblivion to her prey.

But now she is a mother, and she would do anything

for the cubs that mewl softly against her.

Does she know they are too few?

What future is there for

these four fighters?

Four tigers.

Five elephants

travel the dusty paths of memory.

From the day of their birth, the babies walk.

They walk into adulthood and beyond,

following the paths set by their mothers,

who follow the paths set by many mothers before them.

Many miles are covered in the ceaseless search for food and water—

a never-ending journey for these

five travelers.

Five elephants.

Six
Ethiopian wolves

gather on Africa's glorious roof.

There's time for friendly tussles before the day's work begins:

a stern six-mile patrol of their lands

and countless solitary games of "catch the rat."

Later, they will come to rest nose-to-nose to hear and see as one,

not knowing that this rugged world of rock

is the only home for their kind.

Six members of a pack.

Six wolves.

Seven penguins

blink as the storm begins.
Soon, the air will be thick and white,
snow gathering anywhere it can—
on beaks, feet, and the feathers of the young—
so there will be no slippery-bellied slide
into the blue of the sea for fish today.
Just one more huddle in the Antarctic
for these seven survivors.
Seven penguins.

Eight turtles

have traveled an ocean to
return to their birthplace.
Life in the water is what they know best.
The flotilla of females will find the beach,
and they will struggle across thick sand—
making painful progress—to lay their precious eggs.
Then, as if following some ancient call,
they will return to the ocean once more.
A serious journey for these eight migrants.
Eight turtles.

Nine
macaws

perch straight-bodied and chat about their day.

Different squawks say *what* and *who* and *when*.

Strong toes hold up nuts and seeds for hooked beaks to crack.

They seem forever upright, elegant tails pointing at the ground.

Then something startles them and they are

a colorful, fluttering explosion.

Wings ablaze with gold, they flee,

these nine fliers.

Nine macaws.

Ten zebras

know that grazing is thirsty work.

They line up at the waterhole and drink their fill,

ears alert and eyes ever watchful.

Water is the stuff of life itself,

and there are predators that prowl its edges.

Many a sip has been cut short

by the leap of a cat or the snarl of a hyena,

but today remains peaceful for these

ten drinkers.

Ten zebras.

About the animals

One lion
Protection status: *Vulnerable*

The majestic African lion is a symbol of strength and power. Lion numbers have decreased dramatically over the last fifty years because vast areas of grassland where they used to live are now used by humans. Lions living near areas of human activity are often tempted to prey on livestock, leading them into conflict with people. For every three lions you could see in the wild in the 1960s, you can see only one today.

Lions are the most social of all big cats and live in prides that number between four and thirteen individuals. Sometimes one male lion will rule the pride, but often there will be between two and four male leaders. Males protect the pride, marking their territory and chasing off animals that get too close, while females hunt animals such as antelopes, wildebeests, and zebras. A kill will be shared — or squabbled over! — by the pride.

Two gorillas
Protection status: *Endangered*

Mountain gorillas live in thick, tropical forests high in the mountains of Africa, eating a diet of roots, shoots, tree bark and pulp, and fruit. Young gorillas rely on their mothers' care for the first two or three years of their lives and often stay with them for many more. Gorillas are one of our closest living relatives and display a wide variety of behavior that could be considered "human": laughing, playing, and occasionally using tools.

It is estimated that fewer than 900 mountain gorillas are left in the wild; they are found only in Rwanda, Uganda, and the Democratic Republic of the Congo. Their numbers have declined as humans have moved farther into gorilla territory. Recent conservation efforts, however, seem to be reversing that trend.

Three giraffes
Protection status: *Least Concern*

The giraffe is the world's tallest mammal and can grow to a height of nineteen feet. Its long neck allows it to feed on leaves in treetops that most other animals can't reach: its tongue — which is a foot and a half long — plucks off tasty scraps. These distinctive spotted creatures travel across the grasslands in groups to search for food. They are mostly peaceful but males sometimes fight over a female, with battles occasionally ending in injury.

Giraffes in general are not Endangered, but certain species — such as the Rothschild's, or Baringo, giraffe — are. They are hunted by humans for their hides and meat, and their habitats are shrinking as human populations grow and land is cleared for farming. They are also threatened by disease and civil war or unrest. It is estimated that giraffe numbers in Africa have decreased by nearly half since 1999.

Four tigers

Protection status: *Endangered*

Tigers are the largest members of the cat family. Females give birth to two to six cubs at a time, and the cubs stay with their mothers for two years or so before leaving to find their own hunting grounds. During this time, they learn survival skills, such as how to kill prey.

Over the last twenty-five years, tiger numbers have fallen by half. Hunting; forest destruction due to logging, farming, and human settlement; poaching; and conflict with people have all contributed to this decline—and now there are only around 3,000 tigers left. Without this keystone species—predators at the top of the food chain—the populations of large herbivores would increase, putting pressure on plant communities and further disrupting a delicate ecosystem.

Five elephants

Protection status: *Vulnerable*

The African elephant is the largest land mammal; an adult weighs eight tons, which is about the same as four cars. Female elephants live in family groups, or herds, while males tend to roam alone or form small groups with other males. In a female group the matriarch—who is the oldest, most experienced elephant—will use her extensive knowledge and keen memory to lead the other elephants to food or water sources.

Though elephants do not have Endangered status, huge numbers have been hunted throughout the last hundred years. In the 1980s, an estimated 100,000 elephants were being killed every year for their tusks. Though elephant populations in certain parts of Africa are now stable, and some are even growing, in other areas the species remains under threat from poaching and habitat loss as human populations grow.

Six Ethiopian wolves

Protection status: *Endangered*

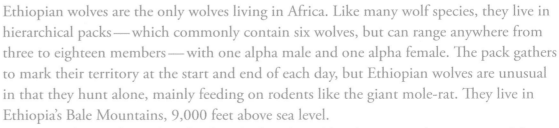

Ethiopian wolves are the only wolves living in Africa. Like many wolf species, they live in hierarchical packs—which commonly contain six wolves, but can range anywhere from three to eighteen members—with one alpha male and one alpha female. The pack gathers to mark their territory at the start and end of each day, but Ethiopian wolves are unusual in that they hunt alone, mainly feeding on rodents like the giant mole-rat. They live in Ethiopia's Bale Mountains, 9,000 feet above sea level.

Numbering fewer than five hundred in the wild, Ethiopian wolves are one of the most threatened carnivores in the world—three times rarer than giant pandas. Their habitat has been eroded because of human population growth in their native Ethiopia. Other threats include disease, like rabies, and hybridization with domestic dogs. Happily, this beautiful creature is now protected by Ethiopian law.

Seven penguins

Protection status: *Near Threatened*

Living in Antarctica, emperor penguins are the only penguins to breed during winter. After laying a single egg, females leave on a two-month journey to feed and to store up food for their offspring, traveling up to fifty miles to reach the ocean. Males stay, covering the eggs with a pouch to keep them warm. At the start of summer, emperors and their young chicks travel to the ocean to spend the summer feeding.

Although this species is not Endangered, the sea ice of the Antarctic Peninsula—where half the world's emperor penguins live—is disappearing due to global warming. This impacts the supply of one of the emperor penguin's main food sources, krill: tiny crustaceans that feed off algae that grows on sea ice. Consequently, scientists estimate that emperor penguin numbers may fall by a third by 2100.

Eight turtles

Protection status: *Endangered*

Loggerhead turtles are the largest of all hard-shelled turtles; they are named for their big heads, and they have strong, powerful jaws. This migratory species follows major currents like the Gulf Stream, and females will travel thousands of miles, often spanning entire oceans, to reach nesting grounds. They come ashore to lay their eggs every two to four years. Sea turtles have been swimming in our oceans for sixty-five million years—witnessing the time of the dinosaurs—and play a fundamental role in marine ecosystems.

Hundreds of thousands of sea turtles are accidentally caught in fishing nets or on hooks each year, and loggerheads are particularly vulnerable because of their migratory habits. This is why, despite healthy numbers in the wild, they have been considered Endangered since 1978. Loggerheads are also threatened by habitat loss, particularly at their nesting grounds on coasts that are being developed for tourism.

Nine macaws

Protection status: *Least Concern*

Highly intelligent, macaws—like the blue-and-yellow species pictured here—gather in flocks, sleeping together in the trees at night and flying long distances during the day to feed on fruit, nuts, and insects. They use loud calls to communicate with one another and to identify different members of the flock. Macaws usually mate for life and form strong bonds, sharing food with and grooming their partner.

Of the nineteen species of macaw, one is extinct, three are Critically Endangered, three are Endangered, three are Vulnerable, and one is Near Threatened, though the blue-and-yellow species pictured here has Least Concern status. Macaws are removed from the wild to be sold illegally as pets and are also threatened by loss of their forest habitat.

Ten zebras

Protection status: *Least Concern*

The zebras pictured here are plains, or Burchell's, zebras, the most common species. They are social animals that live in small family groups consisting of a male, several females, and their young. They will graze on grass and drink at waterholes together, and come to one another's defense in the event of attack by a lion, cheetah, hyena, or crocodile. Each zebra has a unique striped-patterned coat.

Plains zebras range from the grasslands of East Africa to the woodlands of Southern Africa. They are not Endangered but are threatened by overhunting and habitat loss, as human populations expand and take over more land for homes and roads. Other species of zebra are more severely threatened. It is believed that only 2,700 Grevy's zebras remain in Kenya and Ethiopia, giving the species Endangered status.

About the contributors

KATIE COTTON studied English at Oxford University and worked in education before becoming a writer and editor of children's picture books. She lives in London.

STEPHEN WALTON is a self-taught, award-winning artist who works as Supervisor at Bury Art Museum in Manchester, England. His view of art has evolved through his experiences at the museum, where he is the resident photographer. "My artwork developed alongside my love of taking photographs, which resulted in my very particular style and method; when I am out and about I take photographs, and when I am at home I draw from them, although I do also draw from photographs taken by other people. My drawings can take up to a month to complete. I am still finding new ways to use charcoal's qualities and develop my style, and although I do enjoy working in color, I am always drawn back to charcoal to see what else can be achieved with it." Stephen Walton lives and works in Manchester.

VIRGINIA McKENNA started the international wildlife protection charity Zoo Check in 1984 with her husband and eldest son after the premature death of Pole Pole, an elephant she had come to know during the filming of the documentary *An Elephant Called Slowly* and who was later gifted to London Zoo by the Kenyan government. Zoo Check later became the Born Free Foundation. Before getting involved in conservation and animal welfare, Virginia McKenna was a full-time actress, most famously playing the role of Joy Adamson in the movie *Born Free* (1966) opposite her late husband, Bill Travers. She has numerous books to her credit, is a frequent speaker, has traveled extensively, and still accompanies rescued big cats to Born Free sanctuaries in India and South Africa. Virginia McKenna lives in the Surrey Hills, England.

From small beginnings, the Born Free Foundation has grown into a global force for wildlife, taking action worldwide to save lives, stop suffering, and protect endangered species in the wild. Their emergency teams rescue vulnerable animals from appalling lives of misery in zoos and give them lifetime care at spacious sanctuaries. Born Free also runs major international projects devoted to protecting lions, elephants, gorillas, chimpanzees, tigers, polar bears, wolves, dolphins, turtles, sharks, and many more animals, working with local communities to find compassionate solutions so people and wildlife can live together. Throughout all its work, Born Free is committed to preventing individual animal suffering and keeping wildlife in the wild.